Maslow's Hiera
Modern World: Unleashing Human
Potential

Introduction

In the intricate tapestry of our fast-paced and ever-evolving world, where the relentless march of progress never ceases, the quest to understand the intricate workings of human motivation and fulfillment has become more crucial than ever before. It is within this complex realm that the visionary teachings of Abraham Maslow find their eternal relevance, offering us a profound lens through which we can unravel the deepest mysteries of human behavior and potential. Welcome to the captivating journey that lies ahead, as we embark on an exploration of Maslow's Hierarchy of Needs, delving into the very essence of our existence and discovering how this timeless theory resonates and thrives in the vibrant tapestry of our contemporary society.

Nestled at the core of Maslow's transformative theory is the understanding that human beings are not mere spectators in the unfolding drama of life, but active participants, driven by a myriad of needs and desires that shape their every thought, action, and aspiration. With eloquent precision, Maslow's Hierarchy of Needs unveils a framework that illuminates the elemental requirements that propel our species towards self-realization and fulfillment. These needs, stacked in an ascending order of importance, form the bedrock upon which the edifice of our lives is constructed, leading us towards the pinnacle of our human potential.

At the foundational level, we encounter the raw essence of our physical existence. The physiological needs, intrinsic to our survival, beckon us to secure sustenance, shelter, and the nurturing embrace of good health. As we ascend the ladder of needs, the pursuit of safety unfolds, compelling us to forge fortresses of protection in an increasingly interconnected world, where threats and uncertainties loom at every turn. In this tumultuous landscape, the quest for belonging and love emerges as a poignant yearning, beckoning us to seek meaningful connections and cultivate relationships that nourish our souls.

As we ascend further, the significance of esteem takes center stage, urging us to cultivate a deep-rooted sense of self-worth and recognition, amidst the relentless currents of comparison and societal expectations. But the human spirit yearns for more— our innate curiosity and thirst for knowledge beckon us to explore the cognitive realm, expanding the horizons of our understanding and paving the way for intellectual growth and self-discovery.

In the ethereal realms beyond, the aesthetic dimension enchants us, inviting us to immerse ourselves in beauty and creativity, transcending the mundane and basking in the sublime. It is here that the tapestry of life becomes a vivid palette, inviting us to indulge in the harmonious symphony of art, music, and the myriad expressions of human ingenuity.

Yet, the journey of self-actualization awaits, beckoning us to tap into our deepest potentials, unraveling the enigmatic mysteries of our true selves, and sculpting our lives with purpose and passion. This quest transcends the ordinary and propels us towards the extraordinary, as we unravel the layers of our being, discovering our unique gifts, and embracing our authenticity.

But even as the peak of self-actualization seems within our grasp, a profound revelation awaits—the realm of transcendence. Here, we shatter the boundaries of our individuality and reach beyond ourselves, seeking connection with something greater. It is within this sacred space that we bridge the divides of culture, religion, and ideology, unifying the tapestry of humanity with empathy, compassion, and a shared yearning for meaning.

This book, "Maslow's Hierarchy of Needs in the Modern World: Unleashing Human Potential," serves as a guide, unraveling the intricacies of Maslow's timeless theory and revealing its unyielding relevance in the context of our contemporary society. With vibrant narratives, real-life examples, and profound insights, we embark on an odyssey that will awaken your senses, challenge your perspectives, and ignite the flame of self-discovery.

As we traverse the modern landscape, navigating the triumphs and tribulations of the digital age, we will uncover how Maslow's Hierarchy of Needs not only survives but thrives, illuminating the path towards a future where human potential flourishes, where fulfillment becomes a birthright, and where the harmony of our collective aspirations creates ripples of positive transformation in our lives and the world around us.

So, dear reader, embrace the boundless possibilities that lie ahead. Open your mind, open your heart, and embark on this profound expedition into the depths of human nature, as we unravel the mysteries of Maslow's Hierarchy of Needs and unleash the extraordinary potential that resides within us all.

Chapter 1: The Foundations of Maslow's Hierarchy

The life and work of Abraham Maslow

Within the tapestry of human history, certain individuals emerge as luminaries, weaving together the threads of knowledge and insight to illuminate the depths of our existence. Abraham Maslow stands as one such luminary, a psychologist and visionary whose pioneering work continues to shape our understanding of human motivation and self-actualization.

Born on April 1, 1908, in Brooklyn, New York, Maslow embarked on a path that would forever transform the field of psychology. His journey was one of curiosity, intellectual rigor, and a steadfast commitment to uncovering the secrets of human fulfillment. From his early years as a student at City College of New York to his groundbreaking research at Columbia University and later as a professor at Brandeis University, Maslow's insatiable thirst for knowledge propelled him towards new frontiers of human understanding.

Maslow's work was profoundly influenced by his encounters with other prominent psychologists of his time, including Alfred Adler and Max Wertheimer. Their ideas, combined with Maslow's own experiences and observations, coalesced into the revolutionary concept of Maslow's Hierarchy of Needs.

An overview of Maslow's Hierarchy of Needs

At the heart of Maslow's theory lies a profound recognition: that human beings possess an innate drive to fulfill a series of fundamental needs, each building upon the other in an ascending order. This conception gave birth to Maslow's Hierarchy of Needs, a conceptual framework that illuminates the multifaceted nature of human motivation and fulfillment.

The Hierarchy of Needs represents a pyramid-like structure, with each level representing a distinct category of needs that must be satisfied for an individual to progress towards self-actualization and transcendence. It is important to note that Maslow's theory recognizes that these needs are not absolute, but rather exist on a continuum, with varying degrees of urgency and intensity for different individuals.

Understanding the eight levels: physiological, safety, belonging and love, esteem, cognitive, aesthetic, self-actualization, transcendence

At the base of Maslow's Hierarchy of Needs, we encounter the primal realm of physiological needs. These include the necessities of survival, such as food, water, sleep, and shelter. Without satisfying these fundamental requirements, individuals cannot proceed to the subsequent levels of the hierarchy. The physiological needs form the bedrock upon which the rest of the pyramid is constructed, highlighting the intrinsic connection between our physical well-being and our journey towards self-actualization.

Once physiological needs are met, the quest for safety and security arises. This level encompasses physical safety, emotional security, financial stability, and a sense of predictability in one's environment. It is within the sanctuary of safety that individuals can embark upon their personal growth, unencumbered by the burdens of external threats and insecurities.

Beyond the realm of safety lies the yearning for belonging and love, a level that explores the depths of human connection and relationships. Humans are social creatures, driven by an innate desire to form bonds and find acceptance within their communities. This level encompasses friendship, intimate relationships, and the sense of belonging to a group or a broader social circle. It is within the context of love and belonging that individuals find solace, support, and the foundation upon which their self-esteem can flourish.

Esteem, both self-esteem and the esteem of others, becomes the next stepping stone in Maslow's Hierarchy. It is here that individuals seek recognition, respect, and a sense of accomplishment. Self-esteem arises from a deep sense of self-worth, while the esteem of others validates our contribution to society. This level explores the intricate dynamics of identity, self-confidence, and the pursuit of personal mastery.

As we ascend further, the cognitive level emerges, delving into the realm of knowledge, understanding, and intellectual growth. Maslow recognized that humans possess an inherent drive to explore and comprehend the world around them. The cognitive level encompasses curiosity, problem-solving, critical thinking, and the thirst for learning. It is through intellectual pursuits that individuals can expand their horizons, unravel mysteries, and evolve their consciousness.

The aesthetic level invites individuals to embrace the beauty and creativity that permeate their existence. Here, the appreciation of art, nature, and the sensory pleasures of life takes center stage. It is within the realm of aesthetics that individuals find solace, inspiration, and a deep connection to the sublime, transcending the mundane and embracing the enchantment of the human experience.

The pinnacle of Maslow's Hierarchy beckons us towards self-actualization—a state of being where individuals fully realize their unique potentials, embrace their authenticity, and manifest their highest selves. Self-actualization is the profound realization of one's passions, talents, and purpose, leading to a sense of fulfillment and a profound alignment between inner values and external actions. It is a dynamic process, requiring self-reflection, growth, and the courage to confront and overcome obstacles on the path to personal actualization.

Yet, even as individuals ascend to the pinnacle of self-actualization, a transcendent yearning awaits. The level of transcendence encapsulates the profound desire to connect with something greater than oneself—an embrace of spirituality, a quest for meaning, and a recognition of the interdependence and interconnectedness of all beings. It is within this transcendent space that individuals bridge divides, cultivate compassion, and contribute to the greater good of humanity.

As we embark on this profound exploration of Maslow's Hierarchy of Needs, we traverse the intricate landscape of human existence. It is within the realms of physiological survival, safety, belonging and love, esteem, cognition, aesthetics, self-actualization, and transcendence that we uncover the intricacies of human motivation, fulfillment, and self-realization. Through this lens, we gain invaluable insights into the human experience, unraveling the secrets that propel us towards a future where our collective potential can be fully unleashed.

Chapter 2: Physiological and Safety Needs in the Modern Era

In the ever-evolving landscape of the modern world, the fulfillment of our physiological and safety needs takes on new dimensions, as the intricacies of our existence intertwine with the advancements of technology, globalization, and interconnectedness. This chapter delves into the dynamic interplay between our primal survival instincts and the contemporary challenges we face in satisfying our physiological and safety needs.

Examining how our physiological needs have evolved

At the foundation of Maslow's Hierarchy of Needs lies the realm of physiological requirements—the elemental necessities that sustain our physical existence. While the core needs for food, water, shelter, and sleep remain constant, the modern era has introduced new dimensions and complexities to our quest for physiological well-being.

The rapid pace of urbanization and globalization has transformed our relationship with food. We find ourselves faced with an abundance of choices, ranging from convenient fast food options to genetically modified produce. While these developments offer unprecedented convenience, they also present challenges in maintaining a balanced and nourishing diet. The impact of our food choices extends beyond our personal well-being, affecting the health of the planet and the sustainability of our resources. As we navigate these complex landscapes, a growing awareness of the interconnectedness between our dietary choices and the broader ecological and ethical implications becomes imperative.

Similarly, the digital age has redefined the way we interact with the fundamental need for sleep. The constant availability of technology and the allure of screens can disrupt our natural sleep patterns, leading to sleep deprivation and a host of associated health concerns. The ubiquitous presence of electronic devices challenges our ability to disconnect, relax, and prioritize restorative sleep. Striking a balance between the demands of a hyper-connected world and the restorative power of sleep becomes an essential aspect of addressing our physiological needs in the modern era.

Navigating safety concerns in an interconnected world

As our world becomes increasingly interconnected, our safety concerns take on new dimensions. The advancement of technology, while offering unprecedented opportunities, also exposes us to new vulnerabilities. Cybersecurity breaches, identity theft, and digital privacy concerns loom large in an era where our personal information is stored and transmitted across vast digital networks. Navigating these challenges requires a heightened awareness of our digital footprints, the adoption of secure practices, and an understanding of the evolving nature of cyber threats.

Beyond the digital realm, the global nature of our interconnected world demands a nuanced approach to safety and security. Terrorism, geopolitical tensions, and public health crises have become increasingly interwoven with our daily lives, creating a sense of unease and uncertainty. Balancing the need for personal safety with the promotion of open societies and global cooperation presents an ongoing challenge, requiring us to cultivate resilience, empathy, and an unwavering commitment to peace.

Addressing health and well-being in the digital age

The digital age has ushered in an era of unprecedented access to information, connectivity, and technological advancements. While these developments offer immense opportunities for personal growth and well-being, they also present unique challenges to our health and well-being.

The sedentary nature of many modern occupations and the prevalence of screen-based activities contribute to a sedentary lifestyle epidemic. Physical activity, a crucial aspect of physiological well-being, often takes a backseat in the face of demanding work schedules and the allure of digital entertainment. Striking a balance between work, leisure, and physical movement becomes paramount in nurturing our physiological health in the modern era.

Furthermore, mental health in the digital age emerges as a critical aspect of addressing our physiological and safety needs. The constant exposure to social media, the pressure to curate a perfect online persona, and the addictive nature of digital engagement can take a toll on our mental well-being. Cultivating digital literacy, promoting digital detox practices, and fostering meaningful connections in the physical world become essential tools in safeguarding our psychological health.

In the face of these challenges, the importance of self-care and holistic well-being practices becomes magnified. Mindfulness, meditation, and self-reflection offer pathways to navigate the complexities of the modern era, allowing us to nurture our physiological and safety needs in harmony with the demands of our interconnected world.

In the modern era, the satisfaction of our physiological and safety needs assumes new dimensions as we navigate the complexities of technological advancements, globalization, and interconnectedness. By examining the evolution of our physiological needs, addressing safety concerns in an interconnected world, and embracing holistic approaches to health and well-being, we can forge a path towards the fulfillment of these foundational needs. In doing so, we lay the groundwork for the ascent towards higher levels of Maslow's Hierarchy, unraveling the potential for self-actualization and transcendence in the modern landscape.

Chapter 3: Belonging and Love in the Age of Social Media

In the vast digital landscape of the modern world, the concept of belonging and love has taken on new dimensions with the advent of social media. This chapter explores the intricate interplay between social media and our innate yearning for authentic connections, delving into the impact of these virtual communities on our relationships, the challenges they pose, and the opportunities they present.

Exploring the impact of social media on relationships

Social media has revolutionized the way we connect and interact with others, transcending physical boundaries and creating virtual spaces where relationships can flourish. Platforms such as Facebook, Instagram, Twitter, and Snapchat have become integral to our daily lives, serving as windows into the thoughts, experiences, and social lives of others.

These digital platforms offer immense potential for connection, enabling us to bridge distances, find like-minded individuals, and cultivate diverse networks. They provide a platform for self-expression, empowering individuals to share their stories, perspectives, and passions with a global audience. Through social media, we can discover commonalities, foster empathy, and engage in meaningful conversations that transcend traditional barriers.

However, the impact of social media on our relationships is not without its challenges. The curated nature of online personas can create an illusion of perfection, leading to feelings of inadequacy, comparison, and the fear of missing out (FOMO). The pressure to present an idealized version of ourselves can strain authenticity, fostering a culture where superficial connections overshadow genuine intimacy.

The challenges and opportunities of virtual communities

In the age of social media, virtual communities have emerged as powerful platforms for finding belonging and love. These communities bring together individuals with shared interests, passions, or identities, allowing them to connect and form bonds regardless of physical proximity. From online forums and support groups to interest-based communities and professional networks, virtual spaces have the potential to foster a sense of belonging and provide support systems that transcend geographical boundaries.

However, the challenges of virtual communities lie in striking a balance between the digital realm and the physical world. While online connections can offer solace, inspiration, and validation, they may also fall short in fulfilling our innate need for tangible, face-to-face interactions. The superficial nature of online communication can hinder the development of deep, meaningful relationships, making it essential to cultivate a sense of discernment and balance in our digital interactions.

Cultivating authentic connections in the digital realm

In navigating the digital landscape of belonging and love, the cultivation of authentic connections becomes paramount. To forge genuine relationships in the age of social media, we must approach these platforms with intention, mindfulness, and a commitment to nurturing meaningful connections.

First and foremost, self-awareness is vital. Understanding our own values, desires, and boundaries allows us to engage authentically and attract like-minded individuals. By embracing vulnerability and presenting our true selves, we create the possibility for genuine connections to form.

Active engagement in online communities is another crucial aspect of cultivating authentic connections. Instead of passively consuming content, active participation enables us to contribute, share, and engage in meaningful conversations. By actively listening, showing empathy, and offering support, we foster a sense of belonging and forge deeper connections with others.

Moreover, digital detox practices can help us find balance in the digital realm. Taking breaks from social media, setting boundaries around screen time, and engaging in offline activities enable us to reconnect with ourselves and nurture relationships in the physical world.

Embracing the potential of social media as a tool for connection rather than a substitute for it empowers us to navigate the complexities of the digital landscape. By utilizing these platforms mindfully, we can create spaces that foster inclusivity, understanding, and love, transcending the superficiality and embracing the profound possibilities that lie within our grasp.

As social media continues to shape the landscape of our relationships, the quest for belonging and love takes on new dimensions. By exploring the impact of social media on our connections, recognizing the challenges and opportunities of virtual communities, and cultivating authentic relationships in the digital realm, we can navigate this ever-evolving landscape with intention and mindfulness. By embracing the potential of social media as a tool for meaningful connection, we foster a sense of belonging that transcends boundaries and creates a profound tapestry of love in the digital age.

Chapter 4: Self-Esteem and Recognition in the Age of Comparison

In the interconnected world of the digital age, self-esteem and recognition are intricately entwined with the pervasive culture of social comparison and the quest for validation. This chapter explores the profound influence of social media on our self-perception, the challenges posed by online image cultivation, and the importance of redefining success and embracing individuality in nurturing healthy self-esteem.

The influence of social comparison and the quest for validation

In the era of social media, the constant exposure to carefully curated and idealized representations of others' lives has given rise to a culture of social comparison. It is all too easy to find ourselves caught in the never-ending cycle of comparing our achievements, appearances, and lifestyles to those of others. The perceived gap between our reality and the meticulously crafted online personas of others can erode our self-esteem and trigger feelings of inadequacy, leading to a relentless quest for validation and external approval.

The digital landscape amplifies the visibility of achievements, often emphasizing the highlight reel of others' lives. It becomes crucial to recognize that social media provides only a partial and carefully selected glimpse into the lives of others. The illusion of perfection projected online can create a distorted perception of reality, skewing our self-perception and intensifying the pressure to measure up.

Building self-esteem in the era of online image cultivation

In the age of online image cultivation, building and maintaining healthy self-esteem requires deliberate efforts and self-reflection. It becomes imperative to remember that self-worth should not be determined solely by external validation or comparison to others. Authentic self-esteem arises from a deep sense of self-acceptance, self-compassion, and an understanding of our intrinsic worth beyond the realm of digital validation.

Cultivating self-awareness is paramount. By recognizing our strengths, passions, and unique qualities, we can develop a solid foundation of self-esteem that is not contingent upon external factors. Self-reflection allows us to embrace our authentic selves, appreciating the journey of personal growth and progress, rather than solely focusing on the end results.

Another crucial aspect is fostering a healthy relationship with social media. This entails setting boundaries around our consumption and engagement with digital platforms. Mindful engagement involves consciously curating our social media feeds to include diverse perspectives, positive influences, and content that aligns with our values. By reframing our relationship with social media, we can transform it into a tool for inspiration, connection, and personal growth, rather than a source of comparison and self-doubt.

Redefining success and embracing individuality

In the era of comparison, redefining success becomes essential in nurturing healthy self-esteem. Instead of solely measuring success by external markers such as material possessions or societal expectations, it is important to embrace a more holistic and individualistic perspective. Recognizing and valuing our unique talents, passions, and personal growth journeys enables us to define success on our terms.

Embracing individuality is a powerful antidote to the culture of comparison. Each person possesses a distinct set of qualities, experiences, and perspectives that contribute to their authentic self. By celebrating our individuality and acknowledging the beauty of diversity, we can cultivate self-esteem grounded in self-acceptance and appreciation for the rich tapestry of human uniqueness.

It is crucial to emphasize the importance of cultivating a supportive and inclusive online community. By fostering connections based on shared values, authenticity, and mutual support, we create spaces where individuals can uplift and empower each other, moving away from the detrimental dynamics of comparison and competition.

In the age of social media, navigating self-esteem and recognition requires us to navigate the challenges of social comparison, cultivate healthy self-esteem in the era of online image cultivation, and redefine success on our terms. By consciously shifting our focus from external validation to self-acceptance, embracing individuality, and fostering supportive online communities, we can liberate ourselves from the shackles of comparison and nurture a sense of self-worth rooted in authenticity and personal growth. It is through these transformative steps that we can navigate the digital landscape with confidence, cultivating self-esteem that emanates from within and transcends the ever-changing tides of social media.

Chapter 5: Cognitive Growth and Learning in the Information Age

In the dynamic landscape of the information age, cognitive growth and learning have taken on new dimensions. This chapter explores the expanding frontiers of knowledge and the importance of lifelong learning, the role of technology in cognitive development, and the delicate balance between information overload and critical thinking.

The expanding frontiers of knowledge and lifelong learning

The information age has ushered in an unprecedented era of knowledge accessibility and connectivity. The accumulation of knowledge is no longer confined to formal education institutions but has become an ongoing pursuit that spans a lifetime. Lifelong learning has emerged as a fundamental aspect of cognitive growth, enabling individuals to adapt, thrive, and engage with the evolving world around them.

The expanding frontiers of knowledge present us with boundless opportunities for intellectual exploration. Online platforms, digital libraries, and open educational resources provide accessible avenues for acquiring knowledge on a vast array of subjects. The democratization of information empowers individuals to pursue their passions, explore new disciplines, and engage in multidisciplinary approaches to problem-solving and creativity.

Moreover, lifelong learning fosters intellectual curiosity, critical thinking, and a growth mindset. By embracing the process of continuous learning, individuals cultivate the ability to adapt to change, challenge assumptions, and embrace new perspectives. Lifelong learning nurtures a sense of intellectual fulfillment and empowers individuals to become active participants in shaping their own cognitive growth.

The role of technology in cognitive development

Technology plays a pivotal role in shaping cognitive development in the information age. From educational apps and online courses to interactive simulations and virtual reality, technology offers innovative tools that enhance the learning experience and foster cognitive growth.

Digital platforms facilitate personalized and adaptive learning experiences, tailoring educational content to individual needs and learning styles. Artificial intelligence algorithms can analyze data on individual progress, provide targeted feedback, and offer personalized recommendations for further learning. The integration of technology into education democratizes access to quality learning experiences, breaking down barriers of time, location, and socioeconomic status.

Additionally, technology expands the scope of cognitive development beyond traditional educational settings. Online communities and social networks provide platforms for collaborative learning, knowledge sharing, and the exchange of diverse perspectives. Through online forums, individuals can engage in intellectual discourse, contribute to collective intelligence, and tap into the wisdom of crowds.

Balancing information overload and critical thinking

While the abundance of information in the digital age presents unparalleled opportunities, it also poses the challenge of information overload. The sheer volume and accessibility of information can overwhelm individuals, making it crucial to develop skills in filtering, evaluating, and critically analyzing information.

Critical thinking becomes paramount in navigating the vast landscape of information. It involves the ability to discern reliable sources, question assumptions, and evaluate the credibility and biases inherent in the information presented. By honing critical thinking skills, individuals can separate fact from fiction, make informed decisions, and engage in thoughtful dialogue.

To strike a balance, it is essential to develop effective information literacy skills. These skills encompass the ability to search, evaluate, and utilize information effectively and ethically. By cultivating information literacy, individuals can navigate the digital landscape with confidence, avoiding pitfalls such as misinformation, confirmation bias, and echo chambers.

Moreover, mindfulness and self-regulation play a vital role in managing cognitive overload. Developing strategies to prioritize, manage time effectively, and engage in deliberate practice can help individuals optimize their cognitive resources and foster deep learning experiences.

In the information age, cognitive growth and learning transcend traditional boundaries, opening up vast opportunities for lifelong learning and intellectual exploration. Technology serves as a catalyst, enhancing cognitive development and democratizing access to knowledge. However, striking a balance between information overload and critical thinking becomes essential. By cultivating lifelong learning habits, harnessing the power of technology mindfully, and developing critical thinking skills, individuals can navigate the expanding frontiers of knowledge with confidence, harnessing the transformative potential of the information age to foster cognitive growth and thrive in an ever-evolving world.

Chapter 6: The Aesthetic Experience in a Distracted World

In a fast-paced and increasingly distracted world, the pursuit of aesthetic experiences and the appreciation of beauty, art, and creativity play a vital role in enhancing our daily lives. This chapter explores the profound significance of aesthetics, the challenges posed by distractions, and the methods to nurture our aesthetic sensibilities, finding inspiration and meaning in the modern environment.

The significance of beauty, art, and creativity in daily life

Beauty, art, and creativity are essential elements that enrich the human experience. They have the power to evoke emotions, transcend boundaries, and connect us to a deeper sense of meaning and wonder. The aesthetic experience allows us to engage with the world on a profound level, tapping into our innate capacity for awe, inspiration, and self-expression.

Art, in its myriad forms, serves as a powerful medium for storytelling, cultural expression, and social commentary. It invites us to question, reflect, and engage with the complexities of the human condition. Artistic endeavors, whether in visual arts, music, literature, or performance, ignite our imaginations, evoke empathy, and inspire transformative perspectives.

Creativity, too, is an integral part of the human experience. It allows us to transcend the limitations of routine and conformity, fostering innovation, problem-solving, and personal growth. Engaging in creative pursuits nurtures our capacity for originality, curiosity, and the freedom to explore new ideas and possibilities.

Nurturing the aesthetic sensibilities in a world of distractions

In an era defined by distractions, nurturing our aesthetic sensibilities requires deliberate efforts to create space for meaningful experiences. The pervasive influence of technology, incessant notifications, and the demands of a fast-paced lifestyle can erode our ability to fully immerse ourselves in the aesthetic realm. However, by cultivating mindfulness and intentional awareness, we can carve out moments of respite and rekindle our connection with aesthetics.

One approach is to create dedicated spaces and time for aesthetic experiences. Carving out a personal sanctuary at home, visiting art galleries or museums, or engaging in nature walks can provide a respite from distractions, allowing us to focus on the beauty and creativity that surrounds us. By intentionally setting aside time for aesthetic appreciation, we cultivate a deeper connection with our surroundings and our own creative potential.

Mindfulness practices offer another pathway to nurture aesthetic sensibilities. Engaging in mindful observation, savoring the present moment, and developing a heightened sense of awareness can sharpen our perception of beauty and enhance our ability to engage with aesthetic experiences fully. By practicing mindfulness, we become attuned to the nuances and subtleties that exist in the world, enabling us to find inspiration and meaning in the simplest of encounters.

Finding inspiration and meaning in the modern environment

In the modern environment, inspiration and meaning can be discovered in unexpected places. The urban landscape, with its amalgamation of architecture, street art, and cultural diversity, offers a vibrant tapestry of aesthetic experiences. By taking the time to explore our surroundings, we can uncover hidden gems, seek out unconventional sources of inspiration, and engage with the rich tapestry of human creativity that permeates our cities.

Moreover, the digital realm can serve as a source of inspiration and connection. Platforms such as online galleries, creative communities, and virtual exhibitions enable us to engage with a global network of artists, thinkers, and visionaries. By seeking out diverse perspectives and engaging in online discourse, we expand our understanding, challenge our assumptions, and find inspiration in the shared creative endeavors of others.

To derive meaning from aesthetic experiences, it becomes essential to cultivate a reflective mindset. Engaging in journaling, contemplative practices, or engaging in dialogues with others can deepen our understanding and appreciation of the aesthetic realm. By seeking out the stories and narratives behind artistic creations, we unveil layers of meaning that resonate with our own lived experiences and open doors to new perspectives.

In a world marked by distractions, nurturing our aesthetic sensibilities is a powerful means of enhancing our daily lives. By recognizing the significance of beauty, art, and creativity, and intentionally engaging with aesthetic experiences, we tap into a realm of inspiration, wonder, and self-expression. By creating spaces for meaningful encounters, practicing mindfulness, and finding inspiration in unexpected places, we unlock the transformative potential of the aesthetic experience. In doing so, we enrich our lives, connect with our shared humanity, and find solace, inspiration, and meaning in the modern environment.

Chapter 7: Self-Actualization: Fulfilling One's Potential

In the realm of self-actualization, individuals embark on a journey of personal growth, self-discovery, and the fulfillment of their unique potentials. This chapter explores the transformative power of self-actualization, the pursuit of passions and purpose in the digital age, and the methods to overcome obstacles and self-limiting beliefs that hinder our progress.

Unleashing personal growth and self-discovery

Self-actualization is a profound process of unleashing personal growth and self-discovery. It involves delving into the depths of our being, understanding our values, strengths, and aspirations, and aligning our lives with our authentic selves. It is a journey that invites us to transcend the constraints of societal expectations, embrace our unique potentials, and cultivate a deep sense of fulfillment and purpose.

Personal growth and self-discovery unfold through various means. Self-reflection allows us to explore our inner landscapes, unravel our passions, and gain insights into our authentic desires. It is in the quiet spaces of self-reflection that we can tap into our intuition, uncover our deepest motivations, and discern the paths that resonate with our true selves.

Furthermore, embracing a growth mindset propels us forward on the path of self-actualization. Recognizing that personal growth is a lifelong journey, we embrace challenges, view failures as learning opportunities, and embrace the process of continuous improvement. By cultivating resilience and a willingness to step outside our comfort zones, we expand our horizons, discover new facets of our capabilities, and unlock the potential for self-actualization.

Pursuing passions and purpose in the digital age

The digital age has opened up boundless possibilities for pursuing passions and aligning with purpose. Through the power of technology and interconnectedness, individuals can connect with communities, resources, and opportunities that fuel their passions and propel them towards self-actualization.

Online platforms offer avenues for sharing creative work, engaging with like-minded individuals, and accessing educational resources that foster skill development. Social media allows individuals to showcase their passions, reach a wider audience, and connect with potential collaborators or mentors. Crowdfunding platforms provide opportunities for individuals to turn their passions into viable projects and ventures.

Moreover, the digital realm enables individuals to explore diverse interests, experiment with new ideas, and engage in multidisciplinary pursuits. By leveraging online courses, virtual communities, and collaborative platforms, individuals can continuously learn, evolve, and refine their skills, pushing the boundaries of their potential.

Overcoming obstacles and self-limiting beliefs

The path of self-actualization is not without obstacles and self-limiting beliefs that can hinder our progress. These obstacles may include fear of failure, societal expectations, self-doubt, and ingrained patterns of thinking that limit our perception of what is possible.

Overcoming these obstacles requires self-awareness and a commitment to personal growth. It involves challenging self-limiting beliefs, reframing failures as opportunities for learning and growth, and cultivating self-compassion and resilience.

Practicing self-compassion involves treating ourselves with kindness, acknowledging our imperfections, and embracing self-acceptance. By embracing a compassionate mindset, we create a nurturing environment for personal growth, fostering an attitude of exploration and experimentation.

Additionally, seeking support from mentors, coaches, or like-minded individuals can provide guidance, encouragement, and accountability on the journey of self-actualization. These individuals can offer fresh perspectives, share experiences, and help navigate the challenges along the way.

It is also important to celebrate progress, no matter how small. Recognizing and honoring the milestones achieved on the path of self-actualization reinforces a positive mindset and fuels further growth.

Self-actualization is a transformative journey that calls us to unleash our personal growth, explore our authentic selves, and fulfill our unique potentials. By embracing self-discovery, pursuing passions and purpose in the digital age, and overcoming obstacles and self-limiting beliefs, we unlock the profound power of self-actualization. It is through this process that we align our lives with our truest selves, cultivate a deep sense of fulfillment, and contribute to the betterment of ourselves and the world around us. In embracing the quest for self-actualization, we embark on a journey of self-transformation, unlocking the boundless potential that resides within us.

Chapter 8: Transcendence and Meaning in a Globalized World

In a globalized world marked by interconnectedness and cultural diversity, the pursuit of transcendence and meaning takes on a profound significance. This chapter explores the inherent human quest for connection beyond oneself, the challenges and opportunities of bridging cultural, religious, and ideological divides, and the methods to find meaning and purpose amidst the complexities of the modern world.

Seeking connection beyond oneself

Transcendence and meaning often arise from seeking connections beyond the self. Humans possess an innate yearning for something greater than their individual existence. This quest for connection manifests in various forms, such as seeking connection with others, nature, higher powers, or the collective human experience.

Connecting with others enables us to experience empathy, compassion, and a sense of shared humanity. Through meaningful relationships, we discover that our lives are interwoven with the lives of others, fostering a sense of belonging and purpose. By cultivating understanding, embracing diversity, and promoting dialogue, we foster connections that transcend cultural, religious, and ideological boundaries.

Connecting with nature provides a source of awe, inspiration, and spiritual nourishment. By immersing ourselves in the natural world, we develop a profound appreciation for its beauty, interconnectedness, and the intricate balance that sustains all life. Connecting with nature fosters a sense of stewardship and responsibility towards the planet, enhancing our understanding of the interdependencies between humanity and the natural world.

Bridging cultural, religious, and ideological divides

In a globalized world marked by cultural, religious, and ideological diversity, bridging divides becomes essential in the pursuit of transcendence and meaning. The richness of our global tapestry lies in embracing and understanding different perspectives, beliefs, and worldviews.

Bridging divides necessitates cultivating cultural competency, interfaith dialogue, and respectful engagement. By actively seeking to understand and appreciate diverse cultures, we develop empathy and break down stereotypes and prejudices. Engaging in interfaith dialogue promotes mutual understanding, respect, and the recognition of shared values, fostering a sense of interconnectedness and unity.

Moreover, transcending ideological divides requires open-mindedness, critical thinking, and the willingness to engage in constructive discourse. By seeking common ground, finding shared values, and recognizing the complexities inherent in different perspectives, we foster an environment conducive to transcending ideological divisions.

Finding meaning and purpose amidst the complexities of the modern world

The complexities of the modern world can sometimes obscure our search for meaning and purpose. However, it is within these complexities that opportunities for transcendence and purposeful living arise.

Finding meaning and purpose requires introspection and self-reflection. By clarifying our values, passions, and aspirations, we align our actions with what truly matters to us. Cultivating a growth mindset allows us to view challenges as opportunities for learning and personal development, infusing our endeavors with a sense of purpose.

Moreover, actively engaging in acts of service and making a positive impact in our communities and the world around us fosters a profound sense of meaning. By contributing to causes we are passionate about, advocating for social justice, or engaging in volunteer work, we connect with something greater than ourselves and find fulfillment in making a difference.

Recognizing the impermanence and interconnectedness of life enables us to embrace the present moment and find meaning in the here and now. Mindfulness practices, gratitude, and a focus on the here-and-now allow us to savor the beauty, joy, and richness of everyday experiences.

In a globalized world, the pursuit of transcendence and meaning becomes paramount. By seeking connection beyond oneself, bridging cultural, religious, and ideological divides, and finding meaning and purpose amidst the complexities of the modern world, we unlock the transformative potential of transcendence and embrace a sense of purposeful living. It is through these endeavors that we foster compassion, unity, and a deep understanding of our shared humanity. By transcending boundaries, embracing diversity, and finding meaning amidst the complexities of the modern world, we cultivate a profound sense of purpose, fulfillment, and interconnectedness. In doing so, we navigate the global landscape with a sense of awe, wonder, and purpose, contributing to the betterment of ourselves and the world we inhabit.

Conclusion: Embracing the Journey of Self-Realization

Throughout this exploration of Maslow's Hierarchy of Needs in the modern world, we have uncovered the timeless relevance and applicability of this profound theory in enhancing personal and societal well-being. By understanding and addressing our physiological, safety, belonging and love, esteem, cognitive, aesthetic, self-actualization, and transcendence needs, we can unleash the full potential of human beings and foster a flourishing future for ourselves and the world we inhabit.

Maslow's Hierarchy of Needs provides a roadmap for understanding the fundamental requirements that drive human behavior and fulfillment. In the modern era, this framework takes on new dimensions as we navigate the complexities of technological advancements, globalization, and interconnectedness. We have explored the evolution of our physiological needs, the challenges of ensuring safety and security in an interconnected world, the impact of social media on belonging and love, the significance of self-esteem and recognition in the age of comparison, the role of cognitive growth and learning in the information age, the importance of the aesthetic experience amidst distractions, and the pursuit of self-actualization and transcendence in a globalized world.

By applying the insights gained from Maslow's Hierarchy of Needs, we can empower individuals to embrace their journey of self-realization and create positive change in the modern world. It is through recognizing and addressing our core needs that we create the foundation for personal growth, well-being, and fulfillment. When individuals feel secure, connected, valued, and engaged in continuous learning, they are better equipped to unlock their unique potentials and contribute to the betterment of society.

The application of Maslow's theory extends beyond individual well-being to the collective well-being of communities and societies. By prioritizing the fulfillment of fundamental needs at a societal level, we foster an environment that promotes the growth and flourishing of individuals. This includes ensuring access to quality healthcare, promoting safety and security, nurturing inclusive communities that celebrate diversity, fostering a culture of recognition and appreciation, providing opportunities for cognitive growth and lifelong learning, cultivating spaces for aesthetic experiences, and embracing the interconnectedness and shared humanity that transcends cultural, religious, and ideological boundaries.

In embracing the journey of self-realization, we recognize the profound potential that lies within each individual. By nurturing the fulfillment of our own needs, we contribute to the well-being of those around us and the collective fabric of society. As individuals, we have the power to create positive change, challenge the status quo, and shape a future that embraces the values of empathy, compassion, inclusion, and sustainable growth.

Let us embark on this journey together, weaving the wisdom of Maslow's Hierarchy of Needs into the fabric of our lives and the societies we inhabit. By nurturing our physiological well-being, fostering safety and security, cultivating meaningful connections, recognizing our own worth, engaging in continuous learning, immersing ourselves in aesthetic experiences, embracing our unique potentials, and seeking transcendence and meaning, we pave the way for a future that celebrates human potential and fosters a flourishing world.

May each individual find the courage to embark on their own journey of self-realization, unleashing their innate potentials and contributing to a more compassionate, inclusive, and thriving global community. It is through this collective pursuit of self-actualization and transcendence that we have the power to create a future that honors the depths of human potential and brings about a world of harmony, growth, and fulfillment for generations to come.

Epilogue: A New Paradigm of Human Flourishing

As we conclude our exploration of Maslow's Hierarchy of Needs in the modern world, we stand at the threshold of a new paradigm of human flourishing. By integrating Maslow's timeless theory with emerging scientific and philosophical perspectives, we envision a future where individual and collective needs are harmoniously met, and humanity thrives in its fullest expression.

Maslow's theory provides a solid foundation for understanding the fundamental requirements that drive human behavior and fulfillment. However, the advancements in various fields of knowledge, such as positive psychology, neurobiology, and philosophy, offer us fresh insights that can enrich our understanding of human flourishing.

Positive psychology, with its focus on well-being and optimal human functioning, complements Maslow's framework by emphasizing the cultivation of positive emotions, strengths, and virtues. By nurturing positive experiences and embracing character strengths, individuals can enhance their well-being and move beyond mere satisfaction of basic needs towards a state of flourishing.

Neurobiology sheds light on the intricate workings of the brain and its influence on human behavior and experiences. The emerging field of neuroscience reveals the neural mechanisms underlying emotions, motivation, and higher cognitive functions, providing a deeper understanding of how these processes intersect with Maslow's hierarchy. This integration allows us to appreciate the biological underpinnings of our psychological needs and the potential for neural plasticity and growth throughout the lifespan.

Philosophical perspectives, such as existentialism and meaning-centered approaches, delve into the profound questions of purpose, transcendence, and the search for meaning in life. By incorporating these perspectives, we can explore how the pursuit of self-actualization and transcendence aligns with our yearning for a life of purpose, connection, and existential fulfillment.

Envisioning a future where individual and collective needs are harmoniously met, we strive for a world where well-being transcends individualistic pursuits and encompasses the flourishing of communities and the planet. This holistic approach recognizes the interdependence and interconnectedness that exists between individuals, cultures, and the environment.

In this new paradigm, society embraces a collaborative and compassionate ethos that fosters equity, justice, and inclusivity. It prioritizes the fulfillment of basic needs for all, ensuring access to quality healthcare, education, and resources, while also nurturing the growth and development of individuals, recognizing their unique potentials, and providing opportunities for self-expression and contribution.

We envision a future where technology is harnessed ethically and responsibly to enhance human well-being and connection, rather than exacerbate existing disparities. By leveraging technological advancements, we can bridge geographical divides, facilitate communication, and create platforms for collective action and problem-solving.

This new paradigm of human flourishing invites each individual to embark on their transformative journey of self-realization. It encourages the cultivation of self-awareness, empathy, and ethical decision-making, recognizing that our individual actions have ripple effects that extend beyond ourselves. By embracing the integration of knowledge, wisdom, and compassion, we become agents of positive change, contributing to a more harmonious and sustainable world.

As we conclude this exploration, we invite readers to reflect on their own transformative journeys. Embrace the wisdom of Maslow's theory and the insights gained from diverse disciplines. Nurture your physical well-being, cultivate meaningful relationships, explore your passions and purpose, engage in continuous learning, seek connection beyond yourself, and find transcendence and meaning in the tapestry of life.

May you embark on this journey with courage and curiosity, knowing that the pursuit of self-actualization and transcendence is a lifelong endeavor. Embrace the challenges, celebrate the victories, and savor the moments of growth and transformation. In doing so, you not only enhance your own well-being but also contribute to the collective evolution of humanity.

Together, let us envision a future where the fulfillment of our individual and collective needs harmoniously coexists with the flourishing of the planet. As we integrate Maslow's theory with emerging perspectives, we unlock the vast potential of human beings and pave the way for a world where compassion, wisdom, and creativity guide our collective journey towards a more equitable, connected, and flourishing existence.

May this new paradigm of human flourishing inspire us to transcend limitations, embrace our shared humanity, and create a future that honors the depths of human potential. The journey begins within each of us, as we embark on the transformative path towards self-realization and contribute to the creation of a better world for generations to come.

Made in the USA
Las Vegas, NV
07 May 2024

89651481R00031